BOREALIS

BOREALIS

Poems by **Jeff Humphries**
Woodcuts by **Betsy Bowen**

University of Minnesota Press
Minneapolis • London

The University of Minnesota Press gratefully acknowledges assistance provided for the publication of this book by the John K. and Elsie Lampert Fesler Fund.

Published by the University of Minnesota Press
111 Third Avenue South, Suite 290
Minneapolis, MN 55401-2520
http://www.upress.umn.edu

Library of Congress Cataloging-in-Publication Data

Humphries, Jefferson, 1955–
    Borealis : poems by Jeff Humphries ; woodcuts by Betsy Bowen.
        p.   cm.
    ISBN 0-8166-4174-9 (HC/j : alk. paper)
    I. Title.
    PS3608.U57 B67 2002
    811'.6—dc21

                                                    2002003999

Printed in the United States of America on acid-free paper

The University of Minnesota is an equal-opportunity educator and employer.

12 11 10 09 08 07 06 05 04 03 02
    10 9 8 7 6 5 4 3 2 1

CONTENTS

INTRODUCTION ET ALLEGRO

I can still hear you
pour out Ravel, limpid
as water on stones
and in my blood's secret ear
how we made one instrument
just by joining our bodies
to let the northwoods
pour out its music from us,
like light reflecting
ripples on the boathouse walls,
that small fish nearby
shuddered with delight to hear.

VOYAGEURS

He had a vision
and was called visionary.
He saw in his mind
a road to the East,
a royal highway to the
palace of Kubilai Khan,
to gold and spices
and all manner of delight.
For this, he and each
of them burned, even the priest.
Pierre Gaultier de
Varennes de la Verendrye
with four of his sons,
his nephew, a priest, and
fifty *voyageurs*
to haul, row, and navigate
departed from Grand Portage
carrying canoes
and packs into the border
country of the Quetico-
Superior. He

sought the way that is the shape
of everything
he ever could fail to have.
He found beaver pelts,
Indians, an infinite
gloaming wilderness
full of mosquitoes, deerflies,
and ticks, a land of
lichen, moss, and stone, oh stone
of every size
caressed by moss and lichen
of otherworldly
shapes and colors, fungi from
a feverish dream,
from a nightmare, cold beyond
imagining, storms
of snow and rain, wind and hail,
and lakes, a chain of cold lakes
that became the shape
of everything he could
ever fail to have.

He put up buildings
in some places, and gave them
names in his language:
Fort Saint Charles, Fort Maurepas,
Fort Saint Pierre. It did not change
the nature of things.
For eleven years he plied
the watery road
of unrequited desire
with his sons and a nephew,
La Jenneraye, and
Père Mesaiger, and
a troop of men who swore, drank,
and sang lustily
as they paddled, and woke each
day at first light (which
came around four in summer)
to sing and paddle
again, and sleep each night on
stone whose hardness was
not attenuated by
any number of
blankets, awaking each
day to the sounds of
a voice saying *Levez-vous,
messieurs,* and a loon
laughing insanely, and the
staggering vision
of wilderness that stretched on
forever. The men
wanted nothing more than this,
to reenact each
day this splendid debacle
of the heart, this grand
green catastrophe
of failed vision, full of strange
animals and men
who were not at all savage
in their knowledge of
waterways and immenseness,
having lived in the
hollow contours of the white
man's absurd dream for
ever.

He gave up; went home
embittered and ruined, dreaming
of the Khan's palace
rising from a cold, clear lake
surrounded by trees that reached
as far into the distance
as his imagination.

THE LAKE

Vast unblinking eye
that stares forever upward:
earth, reflecting sky
on a cool, dark retina
subtended by fish
and stirred by mammals and birds:
finned feathered furred naked words
that seem to swim or dive or fly.

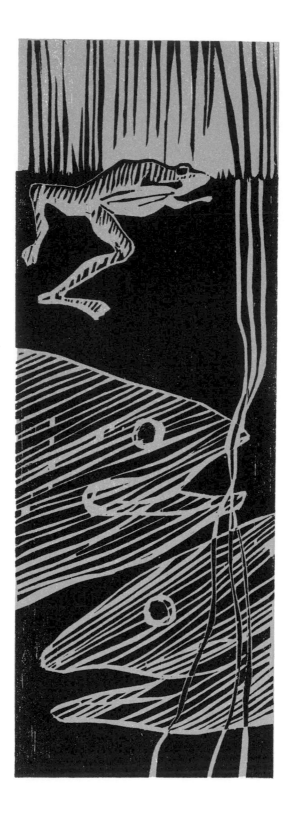

FROGS

In the shallows, half-
submerged among reeds and stones,
where there is a smooth,
dark smell of moss and damp earth,
they speak of water
in a language of water,
clear, brownish-red, green.
The sound of an elastic
band, plucked violently:
the tones vary but tend to
bass, and inflected
by the phlegm of which frogs seem
made. They speak to air
of water, and to the lake
of itself, only
eating the occasional
insect to survive,
and living only to speak
to depths of shallows,
to shallows of glossy depths
where lake trout loll and listen
in their liquid caves
to the vibrations
of the frog's phlegmatic throat,
telling of water
and air, of raindrops and wind,
of loons and their downy young
riding the membrane between,
of the pike that suddenly
pierce it to swallow a voice,
the lake's teeth saying nothing.

THE MERGANSER

The merganser hen
patrols the shore, followed by
seventeen babies,
not all hers. (Other hens laid
their eggs in her nest:
she accepts the eggs and young
of others like her.)
Alone except for the young,
her mate left her when
she began to incubate
in the hollow of
a lichened tamarack snag
leaning from the bank
like an outstretched arm
broken by its fierce, fragile
grip on rock and moss.
A diving duck, her bill is
serrated and hooked
like a gull's, for catching fish.
To the Ojibwe,
the merganser represents
a hardy genius
for surviving cold winters,
while the white hunter
despises it for tasting
like fish. The merganser hen
swims just offshore, followed by
many little mergansers,
some of them hers. Abruptly
she disappears in the lake.
The young turn, emit anxious
noises. She breaks the surface
in their midst, fish in her bill.

MOOSE

Lumbering satyr
grazes near the shore; may sink
entirely out of
view when swimming, then emerge
like Bottom, bestial
fairy-charmed dream of the lake
enfleshed: flatulent,
slack lipped, sad-eyed, receding
chin. His scat tells what
he eats: loose pies from water
plants, hard berries from
upland graze, compressed sawdust
from bark in winter.
Urine is cologne to him;
the females find it
irresistible. In rut
he charges other
males, cars, even trains; may stare
love-struck at a cow
in a farmer's field. When the
dream wears off, he disappears
into woods, or the lake, or
this thin, pale water of words.

OSPREY

On a rock island
blooming from a pine snag
like a huge, charred rose
its nest of sticks defies wind,
assaults of eagles.
In the name of lucent sky
brown and white lightning snatches
scaled tears from the lake's cold eye.

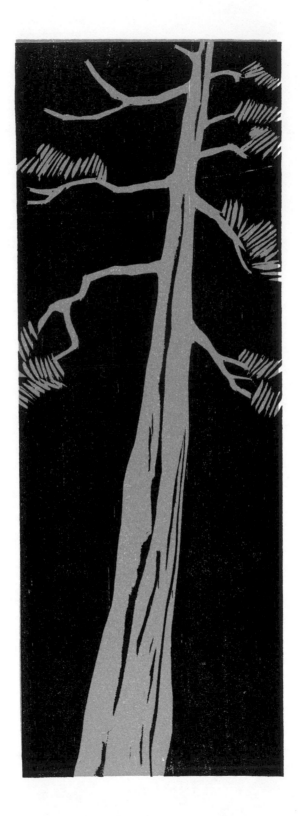

JACK PINE

Dead wood scoured white by
winter snow and wind crown its
Japanese countenance
of green needles and fissured
bark on limbs frozen
in shapes of extravagant
and calm indifference
to inclement elements.

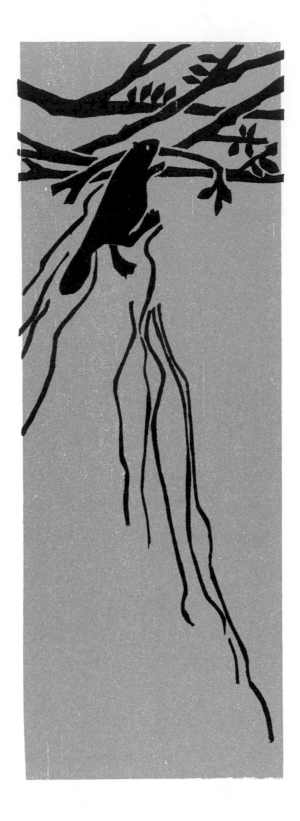

BEAVER

Round brown buck-toothed bark-
eater hides in watery
tent of sticks but leaves
signs: a telltale trail of vees
in the black smooth eye
of the dreaming lake,
low pointed stumps of felled trees
and the sharp, sudden
slap of flat tail on water
that startles loons and sleeping men.

BALD EAGLE

Perfect symmetry
of sky and water, your eye
reflects the lake's vast
lens, encompassing yourself,
a tiny blot lost
on a liquid firmament
that fish, like stars, inhabit.
Your shrill cry reverberates through
northern woods without regard
for the symbols or boundaries
of any nation of men.

ALEXANDER MACKENZIE

One of the partners
of the North West Company,
he inherited
the lust to wander, offspring
of emigrants who
left New York for Montreal
in their loyalty
to King George and Great Britain.
In Canada he
was heir to the dream
of a Passage by
water to the Orient.
It haunted him like a girl
he could not have, and
had never seen in the flesh;
whose body and face
were the shape of perfection.
Alex recognized
the Oriental postures
of stunted jack pines,
the Japanese countenance
of greenstone boulders
hoary with lichen and moss.
He went back to school
in Europe to learn occult
skills of survey and
celestial navigation,
to intercalate
the geographies of space
and human desire,
but they led only to Her
inexorable
absence. He engraved
his failure on a rock face
as he beheld what
might otherwise have been his
goal, the Pacific:

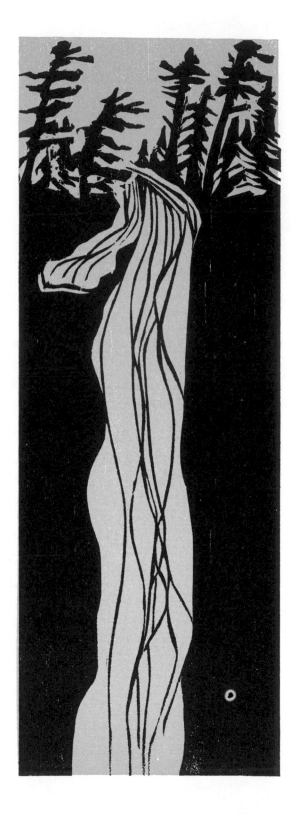

Alex MacKenzie, by land,
came from Canada
the twenty-second July
seventeen and ninety-three.

Near Grand Portage, where
he had started out, between
two resplendent falls,
half of the Brule River
goes down in a cataract
known as the Devil's
Cauldron; so vanished the half
of A. MacKenzie
with his dream of a water
passage to the East,
the same dream that had brought down
so many before.
Now tourists at opposite
ends of his long route
take photographs of themselves
with MacKenzie's words
and the cataract behind
them, inscribing their
failures next to his.

When nine years later King George
knighted him in London, the fire
in his eyes had long gone out.

THE BEAR

No bears in years, the
island's owner told his guest
who feared nocturnal
visitors. But about the

base of a rotten
stump some inquisitor's snout
had poked in pursuit
of squirrel or mouse or grub.

Mink or marten face
would sign earth with a daintier
stroke as it rifled
rodents' houses, and grubs are
not such fine mustelid fare.

At night beneath a
bird feeder hung on a birch
something tore the moss
in search of sunflower seeds.

Conjured by the thought of bear,
fur wet with the lake
he swam across to get here,

he may haunt woods and human
sleep invisible to all
but closed eyes, lit by dark thoughts.

HUMMINGBIRD

Dense fragment of light,
buzz of whose wings heralds flight
of night from the northern woods.

PORCUPINE

He eats wood and fears
nothing, swaddled in a cloak
of brittle daggers.
He has not felt the need to
hurry in so long
he cannot any longer,
waddles over roads
and the large brown eyes look out
of his crushed body
frozen in astonishment
at heedless, rushing
impunity. The fisher
gets a similar
response, flipping him over
to expose tender
underparts. Otherwise, he
is safe in the woods.
He likes to eat the handles
of axes and oars
to get the brine left there by
human hands. He means no harm.

RED SQUIRREL

Smaller and quicker
than grey kin, he is never
still. He swims across
the lake to islands free of
martens and fishers,
his enemies, ricochets
from stump to boulder
like an inscrutable small
force or toy wound up
too tightly. Finding seeds left
out for birds, he spends
the day storing them
one at a time in a stump.
He tolerates not
even his own kind, chucking,
chittering, biting
if necessary. His bites
are calculated.
He is said to castrate greys,
his own only scold
or wound. But when he
swims, may vanish, small russet
note in a green crescendo
of sharp pike teeth closing down.

MAPLE

Flesh blond and tightly
grained enough to blunt the teeth
of saws, its skin is
black and grey on field of white.
The leaves emerge bright
against the immutable
green of conifers,
exploding carmine in fall.
Make a shallow wound,
and its almost clear, thick blood
shed into pails, boils
down to concentrated balm
of the summer woods,
sweet lees of memory or
viscous seed of future spring.

RUFFED GROUSE

Quick brownish-grey birds
the size of banty chickens
haunt the shore thickets.
They appear from nowhere, and
disappear the same
way, bending serviceberry
branches to the ground
with their crops full of ripe fruit.
Everyone hunts them,
wolves, men, martens, hawks, and owls
so they are nervous,
watchful, as they eat green buds
of willow and birch,
blue- and bunch- and red service-
berries, fungi, seeds,
and fuzzy flower catkins
of the aspen trees.
In winter they grow bristles
on their feet so they
can walk on snow, and
burrow into it to sleep,
exploding from drifts
at first light like clods
of brown earth hurled at the sun.
In the spring the male
displays on a stump or log,
fanning his tail and
beating the air with his wings
to make a drumming
sound, raising the crest
on his head, to impress hens.
The hen hides her nest in brush
or tall grass and lays
a dozen tan, brown-streaked eggs.
The campers' dog breaks
five. The saw-whet owl gets one
chick; the raven eats
another. Some hikers find
one, thinking it lost.
They feed it bannock, and it
dies. One afternoon
a weasel kills and eats two

more. The mother leads
two half-grown chicks through wooded
banks of the cool lake,
eating plump berries and bugs,
green buds of aspen and birch,
fattening for winter or
the hunter's gun, hawk, or wolf,
whatever they encounter.
They appear from nowhere, and
disappear just as quickly,
bending twigs of berry trees
with their odd brownish-grey bulk.

MARTEN

Elemental force
careens through branches clad in
brown white and ochre
fur, fanged bolts of ravenous
elegant death hurled
helter-skelter on squirrels:
tree-weasel, dapper
with fox-cunning, mink-
stink, and appetite,
your orange belly means death
to squirrels, money
to the furrier and trapper.

LAKE TROUT

Lake trout lurk in depths
the casual angler cannot
plumb, and lay large eggs
in the bright lap of autumn.
Young emerge beneath
the water's solid winter
face and feed and grow
out of sight in cool water.
Ojibwe women
seined adults in nettle-stalk
nets when they came up
to spawn, then smoked the reddish
meat. Lamprey clamp on
to their sides and suck them dry
as husks, as vacant
as the inside of a word,
like time swallowing
itself, emptying hours from
inside out till just
a rind remains
and the pellucid orange
promise or menace of roe.

RAVEN

Wolves' rude familiar,
imagined by a poet
from south who never
saw you, on silent wings of
stolen night you ride
green dream of daylight, streaking
tamaracks and pines
against blue sky and water
with runes of lugubrious
shape and uncertain import.

THE DROWNED MAN
an autumn campfire tale

The day it happened

The day had been dark,
the sun risen late, and grey,
swaddling the naked
birches and maples, stubbly
green jack pines and yellow
tamaracks briefly with light
soft as owl feathers.

The man it happened to

Ole Hovdal was
self-employed; since the mine shut
down for good he had
worked emptying and stuffing
skins of animals
and fish for summer tourists.
The sky's color, thought
Ole as he lay in bed,
his belly swelling
the blankets between his chin
and his feet, fresh fire
crackling in the iron stove,
the sky's color, scudding clouds
and all, matched the guts
of a pine marten he had
stayed up in his shop till four
to clean. Immobile
forever now, the reckless
prehensile movement
with which it had festooned trees,
like dull lights of fur,
reddish-brown, that flashed almost
imperceptibly
and disappeared, had now been
extinguished, or made
whole, dimensional, and dead.

Taxidermy

Ole had a freezer
full of smallmouth bass, walleye,
and northern pike caught
by big-eyed summer children,
some not over
two pounds, now waiting for his
priestly, grisly hand
like pharoahs or Christians
waiting for Gabriel
on the wall of a cabin,
dead and gaudy, with a lure
hung on their open
mouths like an exclamation.
Some had been frozen
for years now; the wide
dumb hopeful stares of their small
angler-executioners
transmuted during
their frozenness to a smirk
that was distinctly
teenaged, and when they returned
in June or July
to ask if their fish had been
mounted yet, their moms
no longer ever came with.

The wife

He stayed up nights, did Ole,
for day is public
while in the dark, early nights
he could make himself
a yellow cocoon of light
and warmth and whiskey
and indulge the illusion
of calm privacy.
So he slept late through as much
of the scalding light
as he could. His wife, Solveig,
stout, ruddy, and brisk,
would come to the bedroom door
and ask was he dead.

His daughters, and the dark

His three little blond daughters
with hair in pigtails
and round pale blue eyes would come
and play around him
as he lay there, half-asleep,
hearing their tinkling,
nasal chatter through muffling
subterranean
structures of improbable
dreams. He woke to dark
settling in, like a hen loon
on its nest of strange
day-laid eggs, and a sound like
entrails being dumped
in a pan: it was Solveig
cleaning a chicken
for dinner. He rose and washed
himself as little
as he thought he could before
emerging into
the brown, brightly lit kitchen,
with its infinite
rank layers of old food smells,
and decorated
with ceramic effigies
of red chickens, dappled cows,
and pink hogs, a jar
for cookies shaped like a troll,
and badly mended
pine and maple furniture.
His wife was feeling
the need to quarrel, but he
silently demurred,
like an awkward green schoolboy
refusing to dance.

What the man decided to do

Despite the hot smoke rising
from the sauna's stove,
he cranked up the boat
and set out over the lake,
which was almost cold
enough to freeze, and choppy.

The season

The last loon had long
since flown south, the last eagle
climbed the high thermals
out of sight; the bats had hung
their bodies up for winter
or joined flocks of small
birds following summer
to where it withdrew
to hide, and wait out the north
wind's deadly exhalations.
There were no ospreys,
no gulls, only astringent
night air, and the hint
of boreal lights bleeding
their thin and pastel
irregular pulse across
the dark blue expanse
arching overhead.
The lake lay like a fallen
curtain at the base
of a glittering high dome
shot with pink and blue
dust. He leaned over the edge
of the boat and saw
his own face dark and flattened,
frontal silhouette
creased with bright ripples.
A wolf howled, then another.
He set down the rod
and the yellow plastic worm
he had tied to it,
and listened to their plangent,
dissonant music.

Time and water

The difference between air
and water dissolves
in a diaphanous verge,
the precarious
juxtaposition of two
dissimilar but
almost equally flimsy
molecules, making
a surface that is smooth, rough,
or both at once, slick
as any nullity could
be, for it is none
other than nothing, nothing
being the absence
of any thing in the space
between here and now,
and there and then, dry and wet,
cool and warm, cold and
colder, snow and ice, wind and
rain, up and down, wet
and dry: the atemporal
expression of now,
the present instant, which is
the non-time between
the two kinds of time, future
and past, the nothing
we ride from the one toward
the other, never making
any progress till
we get, at last, to The End.
This is nothing but
the skin of the instant, time's
pelt, and we, he thought,
are nothing but its entrails,
but he was so wrong,
for there is nothing within
it, no in to its
out. He leaned, to see himself
better, and fell in.

The water

The liquid cold filled
his sinuses with burning
like a clear molten
lava, and in a short time
also his pale lungs,
from the bottom up; they twitched
like two hares huddled
in a snowdrift, fur parted
by the winter wind.
Strangely his body did
not try to float but
moved easily as a seal
through stone parapets
finally coming to rest
on a bed of green
fronds that, like hands, bore him up.
His wife tried to wake
him with a cup of hot tea
and some lutefisk soup,
but he told her to put them
down on the mossy
stone next to him; he would eat
and drink later but now had
to sleep, he was tired, tired, tired.

The lake sprite

A beautiful girl
came to him through the darkish
sparkling element;
she must be made of water
and cold, but was brown
with limbs and black hair supple
and long as birch trunks
and small dark nipples that squeaked
like rubber against
the ice of his chest, which was
stark white and sparsely
stubbled with small reddish hairs,
for he was naked
all of a sudden, naked

as a jaybird new
born, and her embrace warmed him
though he knew it was
not warmth really, but something
else altogether,
some magic. She was
young enough to be his child
but came from a hot
place inside the cold, and she
was not fair, blue-eyed,
or blond. His daughters sat there
around him, bearing
stunned witness to the water's
embrace of their pa.

The loss of self, or dancing out of time

In the water's embrace he
left the world entire,
skipping lightly, mockingly
over the vapid
dour interval of no-time,
his feet performing
feats of graceful abandon
with ease that was new,
but the lake sprite was leading.
In her charmed embrace
his belly disappeared, years
fell away, till he
was the very spit image
of sturdy Nordic
youth, but light as fairy dust,
for he no longer
had insides to weigh him down,
no in to his out,
none at all, no more than fish
with their guts removed
hung up on a cabin wall,
as light as any
pine marten with its innards
freeze dried inside it
till they were quite ethereal
and superfluous,

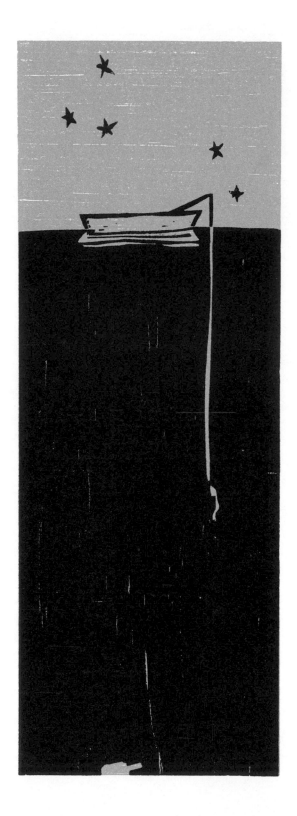

and no difference was there
to tell between in
and out. Ole Hovdal left
the world entire, leaving not
even bones; all they found was
his boat, the empty bottle
of snowshoe grog, but nary
a nail, a hair, or eyelash
of old Ole Hovdal, who
did not exactly die but
found a way to lose himself
in the water's cold embrace.

STONE

Green moss and lichen
stroke immutability
with immobile hands
as it rises from water
crowned by a twisted jack pine.

SAW-WHET OWL

Loose orb of feathers
in a balsam fir: you may
approach him closely
as he rests in brilliant white
midday or gloaming
afternoon; he does not flee
the gaze and footfall
of curious humanity,
rotating his head
so that you and the world are
at once upside-down.

He is mute save for one brief
stint of spring wooing
when the night resounds with him
like a neighborhood
in the city invaded
by trash collectors
at first light, their trucks beeping.

His face at the heart
of the tree, haloed by green
boughs spangled with white,
turns on its neckbone axis
and the world around
it turns like the universe
about a small benign sun.

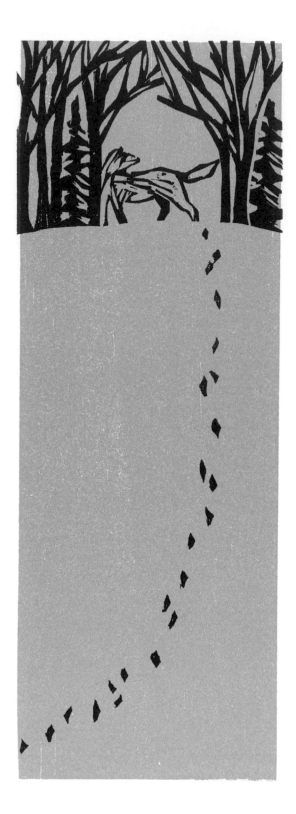

THE WOLF

Old friend, after years
of distance, of knowing you
in books, one of my
own kind has drawn me to woods
that you haunt with her
like the thought of a perfect
thing that is perfectly real.

SONG SPARROW

Three hundred times an
hour he sings variations
on seven or eight
different songs of his own.
But poor singer, your
brood is lost; the brown-headed
cowbird that makes none
itself has found out your nest
of moss and twigs, and laid there
its parasitical egg.

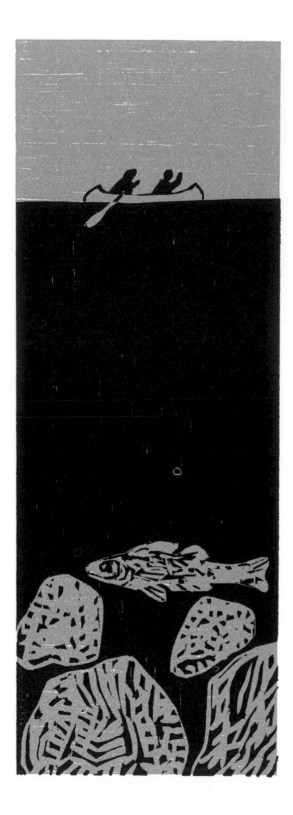

WALLEYE

In the cold water
we drank and used for bathing,
beneath the shiny
black lens of the lake

that our canoe clove
like a slow razor
forming a pearly scar of
ripples, you lurked green

and long among rocks,
perhaps spawning as books say,
without any nest,
devouring minnows, mingling

your wastes with ours in
the liquid element we
shared—so intimate
and yet all I saw of you
was cooked white flesh on a plate.

BIRCHES

Nymphs to the wind's faun,
their white bark elegantly
streaked with shades of black,
they pose at the water's edge
leaning slender trunks
into a cool, lascivious
late summer breeze that makes
their green leaves quiver
like skin lightly touched by skin.

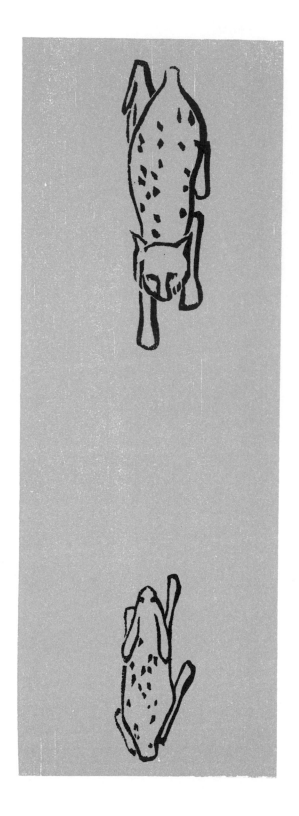

THE LYNX AND
THE SNOWSHOE HARE

In the night forest,
with snow falling, in a copse
of white-festooned trees,
in the cloud-muffled moonlight,
they are locked in an
eternal dance, the hare leads,
the lynx follows. Both
have feet made for the dancing:
broad and furred to stand
on snow and not sink. The lynx
eats hares, culling them.
If the hares decline, the lynx
dances with slow death.
The hare can prosper because
its numbers are held
back from infinity by
the lynx, with its pale
dappled coat and elegant
tufted ears. The hare
wears white or brown according
to season. They stare into
each other's eyes; the cat's are
yellow and hard, the rabbit's
brown and soft. What do they see,
stepping softly over snow
in a clearing of spruces
as the flakes fall, whispering?
Each sees itself reflected
in the other's wide, deep eyes:

A cat and a rabbit are
embracing, stepping lightly.
The cat sinks fangs in the hare's
shoulder, and a bright red cry
cuts through the white, green, and brown
stillness. No one moves. The hare
dies, the lynx lives. The snow falls.

RED-BACKED VOLE

They people the floor
of the boreal wood that
begins where
water sucks gently
at stone, reeds, and pale coarse sand,
whispering secrets
in tunnels that subtend moss
and shallow compost
of fragrant tamarack, fir,
spruce, white and jack pine.
Between the stone, scraped bare by
glaciers, and the sudden fern
and fungi and roots
of trees, are ciphers
hidden from secular view,
read only by voles
and sometimes a weasel who
invades to devour—
in whose dark, hollow runes is
inscribed something calm,
earthy, and ineffable.
It is audible,
however, even to us
in their rustlings and
soft night squeaks and patterings.
Everyone here
devours the voles: coyotes,
hawks, martens, owls, wolves,
foxes, smallmouth bass, toothsome
pike, even shrews who
are smaller, and other mice.
With the voles they swallow what
none of them says but all know,
what is written in careful
brown strokes that never quite dry
though pressed by time and weather
till the meaning is obscure.

LOONS LAUGHING

Night: trees turn to black
sticks against the still lens of
Burntside Lake in which
we are reflected and loons
dive at will, riding
absence of light as though it
were nothing more than
water that the other birds
will drink when the sun comes up.

The wren sings, the dove
coos, but in the brilliant night
of the lake, the loon
laughs at a round rising moon
and what we call love.

Listen rocks stones spoke
language atomic structures
crystal alchemy greenstone
heat pressure moss-
encrusted lichen-choked ea
drop of water voices
greenstone thomsonite
granite schist loon wolf
frog bugs saw-whet ow
they were themselves
words voices that
sometimes saw instead of
hearing sang sparrow
walleye birches leaves
language stones animal
trees birds tents trees
cabin lumberjacks trapper
bear cat snake lake
hare's feet dance lynx s
night cabin girl
glittering lakes fish wi
fire wolves wind northe
igloo snow crystals g
horned owls snowshoe hare
flying squirrels deer mi
red-backed voles scarce
breathing language to pare
the nonsense away nothing
was left truth might
appear in the spaces laugh

THE GEOLOGIST
for Sigurd Olson

Listen to the tale
of a strange man who listened
to rocks, stones, which spoke
to him in a language not
known to his science,
and which frightened him at first.

He had gone to school
for as long as possible
to learn the placid,
obdurate science of stone.

Science means knowledge;
however, he learned nothing
of the language they
spoke (which was not any sort
of proper language
at all, in fact), but only
to look at the rocks
as hard as possible while
without listening,
without hearing, and without
knowing anything
but their atomic structures,
and their putative
places in geologic
time and space, the actual
proper rhetoric
of their crystal alchemy:
from intrusive phase
to extrusive and at length
metamorphic form,
basalt thus turning into
greenstone, which is now
three billion years old, colored
by the mineral
chlorite during its sojourn
underground, in heat
and high pressure, the oldest
exposed rock we know,
which sat naked in his back

Listen rocks stones spoke
language atomic structures
crystal alchemy greenstone
heat   pressure   mass-
encrusted lichen-choked ea
drop of water voices
greenstone   thomsoni-e
granite schist loon wolf
trout bugs saw-whet ow
they   were   themselves
words   voices   that   ha
sometimes saw instead of
hearing sang   sparrow
walleye . birches   leaves
language stones anima s
trees birds tents trees-s
cabin lumberjacks trappers
bear at smoke lake fish
hare's feet dance yr x s wi
night   cabin   guided
glittering lakes fish winter
fire wolves wind northern
lights snow crystals gree-
horned owls snowshoe hares
flying squirrels deer mice
red-backed voles scarcely
breathing language to pare
the nonsense away nothing
was left truth might
appear in the spaces laugh

yard in Ely where
it had sat naked for three
billion years and spoke
in a bright, moss-encrusted,
lichen-choked voice what were not
noises, properly
speaking, not noises at all,
that is, no one heard
them but him, and he did not
hear them exactly
himself, not in fact by dint
of any sound waves
striking the drum of his ear.

Near the Laurentian
Divide, from which the same drop
of water will run
east or west, the difference
depending only
on which side it falls,
near this crux of opposite
forces, in the wild
border country, infested
by silence and strange
voices of spirits that had
never existed,
the greenstone and Thomsonite
the granite and schist
spoke to him in cool, deep tones
inflected by age
so great that it was only
a meaningless abstraction.
So did loon and wolf,
not by laughing or howling,
so did the sleek trout,
but not in the sucking noise
it made eating bugs,
so did the saw-whet owl, not
in the twanging call
of the male as he seduced
the she saw-whet; these
were secondary effects.
It was not even
so much that they spoke as that

Listen rocks stones smoke
language atomic structure;
crystal alchemy greenstone
heat   pressure   moss-
encrusted lichen-choked earth
drop   of   water   voices
greenstone   thomsonite
granite schist loon wolf
trout bugs saw-whet owl
they   were   themselves
words   voices   that   he
sometimes saw instead of
hearing sang spoke
walleye . birches leaves
language stones animals
trees birds tents faces
cabin lumberjacks trappers
bear . at smoke lake fire
hare's feet dance lynx springs
night   cabin   guide
glittering lakes fish winter
fire wolves wind northern
lights snow crystals great
horned owls snowshoe hares
flying squirrels deer mice
red-backed voles scarce
breathing language to pare
the nonsense away nothing
was   left   truth   might
appear in the spaces laugh

they were themselves words,
voices, that he sometimes saw
instead of hearing.
They did not look like
print on a page, but simply
like a wolf, a loon,
a small owl, or song sparrow
with its infinite,
or nearly, variations
on a theme, the white
flesh of a walleye he fried
in the woods after
catching, the birches' rustling
leaves that turned golden
before they fell to the ground.
These were a language
that did not mean anything
but itself, themselves.
In the din of his fellow
humans' company,
he could not often hear it
or see it at all
though he saw stones, animals,
trees, and birds, though he
tried hard to hear it,
which was also to see it,
but they did not let
him save when he was alone.

He stayed up all night
in tents in the cool forests
keening to the sounds
of their boreal presence.

In a cabin left
by lumberjacks or trappers
long ago that reeked
still after decades empty
of bear fat and smoke,
overlooking a small bay
of the lake, he kept
a vigil all night alone.
The fire extended
prehensile yellow and red

Listen rocks stones spoke
language atomic structure
crystal alchemy greenstone
heat pressure moss-
encrusted lichen-choked ear
drop of water voices
greenstone thomsonite
granite schist loon we
trout bugs saw-whet owl
they were themselves
words voices that me
sometimes saw instead of
hearing sang sparrow
walleye . birches leaves
language stones animals
trees birds tents forests
cabin lumberjacks trapper
bear cat smoke lake fire
hare's feetdance lynx snow
night cabin guides
glittering lakes fish winter
fire wolves wind northern
lights snow crystals gre
horned owls snowshoe hares
flying squirrels deer ni
red-backed voles scarce,
breathing language to pare
the nonsense away nothing
was left truth might
appear in the spaces. laugh

appendages up
the gaping flue's mouth,
making weird shadows flicker
on the walls, and they
came close around him, voices,
in a widening
circle, cackling and heaving,
dancing to obscure
rhythms that he was disturbed
to find that he knew
but could not have heard before.
At times he became
afraid, and cried out, and they
would disappear for a while,
and it should have been
peaceful but was not at all.
He learned finally
to keep silent, and that no
apparatus could
record them in photographs
or magnetic tape,
for they were not images
or noises a machine would
recognize, just as
they were not reducible
to any effect
like the loon's laughing
or the hare's feet as it danced
its brief bloody dance
with the lynx in new fallen
snow that made a dull
crunching noise underneath them.

Nor were these fairies
or elves that crowded around
him in dark winter
and clear green days of summer,
not at least as he
had learned to conceive fairies
and elves, but perhaps
as the old Celts had known them.

He stayed up all night
in the cabin on the point,

Listen rocks stones spoke
language atomic structures
crystal alchemy greenstone
heat pressure moss-
encrusted lichen-choked earth
drop of water voices
greenstone thomsonite
granite schist loon wolf
trout bugs saw-whet owl
they were themselves
words voices that he
sometimes saw instead of
hearing song sparrow
walleye . birches leaves
language stones animals
trees birds tents faces
cabin lumberjacks trappers
bear fat smoke lake fire
hare's feet dance lynx snow
night cabin grief
glittering lakes fish wind
fire wolves **wind** northern
lights **snow crystals** great-
horned owls **snowshoe hares**
flying squirrels deer mice
red-backed **voles** scarcely
breathing **language to pare**
the nonsense away nothing
was left **truth** might
appear in the spaces **laugh**

sober though with drink
close by, and he bore witness
to these things that made
no sense to him whatever.

In winter he taught
to others what he had learned
about rocks in schools
from learned men—a great deal,
but not much; still he
dared not reveal the stones' dense,
obscure dialect,
the dry, homely obdurate
truths they had told him.
In the summer he guided
tourist-fishermen
in canoes through the cool chain
of glittering lakes
that led toward Hudson's Bay,
and polar tundra,
following old voyageurs'
and trappers' highways
through clear, deep water that teemed
with fish of good size.
Sometimes the fishermen who
hired him became friends.
He dared not tell them either.
In the white silence
of the winter evenings,
he sat by the fire
with the wolves and wind howling
outside, and northern
lights casting reflections, pink
and blue, in the soft
snow crystals that had fallen
suddenly, he listened
to a pair of great horned owls
whose booming hoots made
every small thing alive
and awake shudder,
snowshoe hares, huge-eyed
flying squirrels and deer mice,
red-backed voles that stopped

Listen rocks stones spoke
language atomic structures
crystal alchemy greenstone
heat pressure moss-
encrusted lichen-choked ear
drop of water voices
greenstone thomsonite
granite schist loon wolf
trout bugs saw-whet owl
they were themselves
words voices that he
sometimes saw instead of
hearing song sparrow
walleye birches leaves
language stones animals
trees birds tents foxes
cabin lumberjacks trappe
bear cat snake lake fire
hare's feet dance lynx sho
right cabin guid
glittering lakes fish win
fire wolves wind nort
lights snow crystals great
horned owls snowshoe hares
flying squirrels deer mice
red-backed voles scarce
breathing **language to pare**
the nonsense away nothing
was left **truth** might
appear in the spaces **laugh**

and held still scarcely breathing
in their galleries
that riddled the earth and snow.

In this frozen silence fraught
with signs, he would tap
with his fingers on a box
in which marks appeared
on a rolled sheet of paper.
He would tap and tap
and listen, and what came out
was not what he had
heard, and not what he had seen.
But sometimes, there was
a small inkling of something
that at length he learned
to distinguish from the rest.
It was hard to see
as any hare in the snow
with its perfect white
and black on the tips of ears
looking like nothing,
nothing at all, till it moved.
Something of what he
had seen and heard lay hidden
among flaccid dross
of ordinary language
that was all over
like moose droppings in summer
when the great beasts eat
water plants and their bowels
are gassy and loose.
He tapped and banged, and listened,
and tapped some more till
among the loose piles of dreck
he began to see
a certain meaning, and tried
to pare the nonsense
away, leaving only sense,
but then nothing was
left, nothing for every
thing had been crossed out.
So he discovered he had
to keep a certain

Listen rocks stones spoke
language atomic structures
crystal alchemy greenstone
heat pressure moss-
encrusted lichen-choked ear
drop of water voice
greenstone thomson
granite schist loon wolf
trout bugs saw-whet owl
they were themselves
words voices that he
sometimes saw instead of
hearing song sparrow
walleye birches leave
language stones animal
trees birds tents forests
cabin lumberjacks trapper
bear fat smoke lake fire
hare's feet dance lynx sno
night cabin guided
glittering lakes fish winter
fire wolves wind northern
lights snow crystals great
horned owls snowshoe hares
flying squirrels deer mice
red-backed voles scarcely
breathing language to pare
the nonsense away nothing
was left **truth** night
appears in the spaces **laugh**

quotient of impurity
in order that truth
might appear in the spaces.
The key was to know
what to leave, and what to cross
out, for without its
laugh, the loon was not a loon,
and without its song,
the sparrow was not a bird
though these were only
effects, and not the true thing.

So this middle-aged
man became a conjurer
decried by many
as a lunatic who saw
and heard things that were
not real, and worshiped false gods,
the simple deities
of moss, tree, stone, fish, feather,
and fur, which appeared
to him when he was alone.

JEFF HUMPHRIES lives and writes in New Orleans. He wrote these poems during his frequent visits to Burntside Lake near Ely, Minnesota, not far from Sigurd Olson's Listening Point. He is the author and editor of twelve previous books, including *A Bestiary,* a collection of poems.

BETSY BOWEN, an award-winning artist, makes woodblock prints on the north shore of Lake Superior in Grand Marais, Minnesota, where she operates Betsy Bowen Studio, a fine art family print shop. She is the author and illustrator of *Antler, Bear, Canoe: A Northwoods Alphabet Year, Tracks in the Wild,* and *Gathering: A Northwoods Counting Book.*